To learn more about Jeff, visit:

https://jeffarnold.com

https://www.linkedin.com/in/rjefferyarnold

Also By Jeff:

The Art of the Insurance Deal

How to Beat Your Insurance Company

Tech-Forward, Tech-Enabled or Tech Shackled: Which Are You?

Insurance Evolved: INSURANCE 2025

Moments With Mucka: Business Building Sessions

MONEY SECRETS

A Little Book of Wisdom

Jeff Arnold

Copyright © 2022

Published by Jeff Arnold

PRINTED IN THE UNITED STATES OF AMERICA

102022

All rights reserved. Without limiting the rights under copyright reserved above, no part of this book may be reproduced, stored or introduced into a retrieval system, or transmitted, in any form or by any means (electronic, mechanical, photocopying, recording or otherwise), without the prior written permission of both the copyright owner and the publisher.

DISCLAIMER: THIS BOOK IS NOT LEGAL ADVICE

This book contains the opinions and ideas of the author. The purpose of this book is to provide you with helpful information. This book should not be construed as legal advice for your specific situation since each individual situation is unique. Any suggestions in this book should be followed with the advice of appropriate financial and legal counsel.

Contents

Introduction 1

What's This Book All About?............................3

What Is an Heir, Heiress & Inheritor?..............5

SECRET #1: The Rule of 72 9

SECRET #2: The 4% Rule 13

SECRET #3: Dividends 17

SECRET #4: Compounding Value 21

SECRET #5: Money Listens and Obeys..........25

SECRET #6: Interest: Friend or Foe...............29

SECRET #7: Credit, Credit Cards & Credit Lines 33

SECRET #8: Money Talks; Wealth Whispers. 37

SECRET #9: Be Your Own Bank....................41

SECRET #10: Transferring Wealth 45

SECRET #11: Stealth Wealth..........................49

SECRET #12: Annuities: SPIA........................53

SECRET #13: Annuities: SPDA 57

SECRET #14: Taxes 61

SECRET #15: Build Your Own
Wealth Transfer Blueprint.............................. 65

Ways to Work With Me & RIGHTSURE 69

About Jeff Arnold.. 71

About RIGHTSURE 73

Other Books by Jeff Arnold 75

This book is dedicated to my children, grandchildren, and anyone looking to leave an inheritance for the next generation.

Introduction

Four Seasons Residence Club
Carlsbad, CA

The chatter around the Four Seasons today is remarkably similar to every other day. People are gathered at nearby tables discussing family and business, and as is often the case in five-star, high-end resorts, conversations often turn to the subject of money.

I am speaking about money in the form of inheritances, trusts, heirs, heiresses, and estate distributions, and a host of conversations that many in the world are not privy to.

The conversations that the upper middle class, the rich, and the wealthy have about money are often very different when compared with one another. As we will soon discuss, Money Talks; Wealth Whispers. And at Four Seasons, many are whispering.

During a multi-hour lunch meeting with a brilliant economist, we engaged in deep conversation surrounding how we are currently witnessing the greatest wealth transfer in the history of mankind and how so many inheritors are ill-prepared to receive, use and deploy their newfound riches.

It was at the end of the luncheon that I was compelled to write this primer that you now hold in your hand.

After decades of being "inside" the lives of heirs, heiresses, and an expansive circle of inheritors, I have consolidated what I believe to be some very important concepts and simple principles of knowledge you should embrace relative to money and the rules for using it, which in the end, will help you identify your own wealth transfer superpower.

What's This Little Book All About?

This little book, also called a primer, has been strategically designed and thoughtfully curated to introduce you to some relevant concepts.

The chapters are intentionally "twitterized" to contain short subject introductions, followed by a brief overview, a "What you Should Know" section (quick history lesson) and a "What you Should Do Now" action plan.

Lastly, each chapter will end with a quote that correlates to that section's concepts.

When you close this primer, you will have an understanding of how to make your money work for you while giving you great confidence in navigating your life.

Oh, and one final thing: You will also possess the knowledge and have a road map to creating and transferring your own wealth.

Heirs, Heiresses, & Inheritors

What is an Heir, Heiress & Inheritor?

Firstly, for purposes of this book, let us agree that the words, heir, heiress, and inheritor reflect the summaries below.

HEIR

An heir is a person who inherits or will potentially inherit property from another.

HEIRESS

An heiress often refers to a female heir, the beneficiary of an inheritance.

INHERITOR

An inheritor is a person who receives money, property, or assets from someone who has died.

While many individuals I have met or worked with would never consider themselves an heir or heiress, once they are presented with these definitions, we mutually agree that they are now the recipient of this title.

I submit to you, it is also true that most people have visions of an heir, heiress, or inheritor as uber wealthy or the recipient of millions or billions in assets, but the reality is, even if you are due to inherit your grandparents' savings, parents' home, or a great-uncle's investment account, either way, you are now considered an heir.

> "We are all gifted.
> That is our inheritance."
>
> ~ Ethel Waters~

SECRET #1:

The Rule of 72

The Rule of 72 is a simplified formula that calculates how long it'll take for an investment to double in value, based on its rate of return.

What You Need to Know

Being that you were most likely gifted shares of stock, a recipient of a trust fund, or granted a monthly allotment of cash each month, you often view money differently.

The mindset of most heirs I speak to regarding money is:

"It's always been there for me."

Likewise, some heirs receive a small amount of money that they would like to make grow into a much larger amount of money. Their mindset is:

"How do I make this inheritance grow?"

I challenge both groups of these inheritors by asking two simple questions.

What if you could make your money double?

What would it take to double your inheritance and have even more?

The History

The Rule of 72 dates back to 1494 when Luca Pacioli referenced the rule in his comprehensive mathematics book called *Summa de Arithmetica*.

What You Should Do Now

If you are looking to double your inheritance, you must understand the simple Rule of 72 Formula.

Divide 72 by the expected rate of return. 72/10 = 7.2 years to double your money.

EXAMPLE 1: If your bank is offering you 1% on your money, it will take 72 years for your money to double.

EXAMPLE 2: If your favorite stock or fund is earning you 20% on your money, it will take 3.6 years to double your money.

EXAMPLE 3: If your research locates a hidden gem of an investment that earns you 36% returns, it will take 2 years to double your money.

"If you want to build or transfer generational wealth, you must understand the rule of 72."

~ Jeff Arnold ~

SECRET #2:

The 4% Rule

The 4% Rule seeks to establish a steady and safe income stream that will meet current and future financial needs. Simply stated, the 4% Rule suggests you withdraw no more than 4% of your total savings or inheritance amount.

What You Need to Know

You have most likely sat down with your trust officer, banking executive or a member of your family's "family office."

They could have used some very big, very confusing words about a maximum amount you can access of your trust or inheritance, etc.

Much of this is because your benefactor wanted your money to outlive you or at the least be there your entire life.

To extend the life of your inheritance, you need to understand how the 4% Rule works.

What happens if you ignore the 4% Rule, raid your trust, depleting it of cash?

Violating the 4% Rule in a single year to splurge on a major purchase can have severe consequences down the road. Once you begin to devour your assets' principal amount, your future 4% withdrawals will have to be reduced, or you will run out of money faster. You have no doubt heard stories of heirs who blew through their fortunes in record time. If only they understood the simple 4% rule.

The History

In 1994, using historical data on stock and bond returns over a 50-year period (1926 to 1976), financial advisor, William Bengen, challenged the previous go-to thinking that withdrawing 5% yearly in retirement was a safe bet.

What You Should Do Now

While the 4% Rule was created for retirees to gauge lifelong payouts, it is a most valuable formula to help your inheritance last you 20 to 30 years.

Understanding the 4% Rule is pivotal to keeping your money working for you.

Example 1: A 100,000 inheritance should take no more than $4,000 per year in distributions.

Example 2: A 400,000 inheritance should take no more than $16,000 per year in distributions

Example 3: A $1,000,000.00 inheritance should take no more than $40,000 per year in distributions.

"If you buy things you do not need, soon you will have to sell things you need."

~ Warren Buffet ~

SECRET #3:

Dividends

A dividend is the distribution of corporate earnings to eligible shareholders.

What You Need to Know

It is highly probable that much of your income is derived from dividends of stocks placed in your trust.

While not all companies pay dividends, those companies that do, usually reinvest back into the company to make its stock perform better, thereby increasing stock prices and your investment.

Example of a Dividend:

If a company's board of directors decides to issue an annual 5% dividend per share, and the company's shares are worth $100, the dividend is $5. If the dividends are issued every quarter, each distribution is $1.25.

The History

In financial history of the world, a Netherlands firm, called the Dutch East India Company, was the first recorded (public) company ever to pay regular dividends.

What You Should Do Now

The talk surrounding dividends might not possess the awesomeness of say, crypto or some high-tech stock, but over time by making sure you have some of your investments in dividend-based stocks, you will be delighted with the returns.

The power of dividends and their compounding effect is an important and vital principle to understand.

"Do you know the only thing that gives me pleasure?

It is to see my dividends coming in."

~ John D. Rockefeller ~

SECRET #4:

Compounding Value

(Sometimes Called
Time Value of Money)

Compounding may occur on investments where savings grow more quickly or on debt where the amount owed may grow even if payments are being made.

What You Need to Know

The primary thing I tell heirs about compounding is, "It can work for you and most definitely can work against you."

"It can make you a master, or you can become its slave; the choice is yours alone."

The History

Once referred to as the eighth wonder of the world by Albert Einstein, compounding and compound interest play a very important part in shaping the financial success of investors.

If you take advantage of compounding, you'll earn more money faster.

If you take on compounding debt, you'll be stuck in a growing debt balance longer.

What You Should Do Now

Buy one share of a dividend-paying stock, and watch it compound with amazement as your money increases even while you are sleeping.

Alternatively, sign up for a credit card with a high interest rate, and watch your money quickly leave your bank account faster than you can make it back.

I would like to end this chapter with a statement made to me over a lunch with Hunter Hastings. In speaking of compound interest, he remarked, *"When it comes to compounding, do a lot of the good kind and very little or none of the bad."*

To learn more about Hunter Hastings' work, visit: https://hunterhastings.com.

"Compound interest is the eighth wonder of the world. He who understands it, earns it. He who doesn't, pays it."

~ Albert Einstein ~

SECRET #5:

Money Listens and Obeys

Your money will do exactly as you instruct it to do.

What You Need to Know

The greatest thing about money is that it will do exactly as you tell it to.

If you inform your money that you wish it to go forth, produce a return and provide you with even more—it will comply.

Likewise, if you tell it that you don't care about it and squander it, spend it foolishly or use it to impress others—it shall quickly, rapidly dissolve and leave you to find another who will master it.

The History

There is a saying that "Money talks and wealth whispers." This has been true throughout the ages.

What You Should Do Now

Tell your money to make more money for you. One of the great delights in my life is having heirs be consistently well versed and able to dialogue with me about what they are telling their money to do.

Show your money that you are paying attention by tracking where it goes, monitoring who it goes to, reigning in fees and interest payments and applying expense reduction exercises constantly.

In so many instances when heirs can discuss the concepts in this book without reservation or timid behavior, I become convinced that the gift bestowed upon them will accomplish much and their benefactors (wherever they may be) are smiling upon them.

> "Your money needs direction. If you want more from your money, you need to tell it what to do and where to go."

~ Some Really Smart Person ~

SECRET #6:

Interest: Friend or Foe

Interest is a fickle, fickle thing. It can be your very best friend or your most ardent adversary. The poor pay interest, while the rich earn interest.

What You Need to Know

Interest is either the price you pay for credit you are using or the amount of money you are earning on deposited money.

If you are borrowing, it is prudent to know how the interest will be compounded, and likewise, if you are earning interest, always seek the highest amount with the least risk.

The History

The first recorded instance of credit is a collection of old Sumerian documents from 3000 BC that show systematic use of credit to loan both grain and metals.

What You Should Do Now

It is quite interesting that all religions have many quotes, verses and sub contexts surrounding interest, and I highly encourage you to study them.

As for you using interest to buy things, like cars, houses, gifts, etc., prior to any big purchase, I urge heirs to seek guidance from others in their circle and definitely from their advisors.

Often this guidance is not sought because the answer could be one that they do not wish to hear.

Your advisors are to advise you; it is your job to make prudent, wise, reflective decisions.

Remember, the goal is to be earning interest (good) not paying interest (bad).

"Interest that you pay is a penalty. Interest that you earn is a reward."

~ Chris Hogan ~

SECRET #7:

Credit, Credit Cards, & Credit Lines

Credit, credit cards, and credit lines involve a contract agreement in which a borrower receives a sum of money or something of value and repays the lender at a later date, generally with interest.

What You Need to Know

When you use credit, via a credit card, a credit line, margin interest on your brokerage account, etc., it is the same as taking a loan.

Using credit generally means you borrow money to buy something.

- You borrow money (with your credit card or a loan).
- You buy the thing you want.
- You pay back that loan later—with interest.

The History

Origins of credit and modern consumer credit.

3,500 BC—Sumer

Sumer was the first urban civilization, with about 89% of its population living in cities. It is thought that here consumer loans, used for agricultural purposes, were first used.

1803—England

Credit reporting itself originated in England in the early 19th century. The earliest available account is that of a group of English tailors that came together to swap information on customers who failed to settle their debts.

What You Should Do Now

Most heirs begin their credit journey in their late teens when they access funds to buy vehicles, pay for college or start businesses.

Oddly enough, most of the inquiries I hear revolve around what credit card they should get, to which my common reply is, the one with the lowest limit, forcing you to pay it off in-full monthly to help increase your credit score if you need to borrow in the future.

When it comes to interest, there are only two kinds. Bad Interest is money you pay, "Interest at work through the institution of credit."

Good interest is money paid to you through savings and investments.

> "Credit card interest payments are the dumbest money of all."

~ Hill Harper ~

SECRET #8:

Money Talks; Wealth Whispers

If you listen closely, it becomes easy to hear the difference.

What You Need to Know

The simple difference between a rich person and a wealthy person is that a wealthy person has sustainable wealth. In other words, a wealthy person will always be wealthy, whereas someone who is merely rich will only be so for a short period of time until the money is gone.

The History

Wealth and inheritance have been around forever. The families and heirs who perpetuate generational wealth are the ones who understand and use nearly all of the simple principles in this book.

What You Should Do Now

Listen to your money; it's telling you it wants to work harder for you but wants direction.

There exists a great many platforms that provide some candid, eye-opening discussions around the statement, "Money talks; wealth whispers."

Mastering the first four principles of this primer offers a solid head start to join the whispering crowd versus the loud talking one.

Your money is always speaking to you, but you have to be listening. You prove you are listening by limiting its outflow and being diligent about putting it to work.

A billionaire friend of mine begins each morning sitting in silence with his morning coffee, listening, being reflective and literally having a conversation with his money, telling it, "Work hard today. Do not be foolish. And close today with adding value to my estate."

In a hush "whispered" voice, I say to you, "Hello friend, may you begin to see yourself as wealthy and not rich."

> "Wealth is quiet.
> Rich is loud.
> Poor is flashy."

~ A Pinterest Post I Saved ~

SECRET #9:

Be Your Own Bank

Many heirs and heiresses have the instant ability to quite literally *be their own bank*.

What You Need to Know

Becoming your own bank isn't a new strategy. In fact, people have been using a simple legal contract called life insurance as a bank dating back before the Civil War.

It's even built into the U.S. tax code and receives favorable treatment by the IRS. Today's best policies are backed by top-rated mutual insurance companies and can be customized with more options than ever before to fit your financial goals and budget.

There is much to learn regarding using life insurance as a bank to grow and protect your wealth. Here is a six-step simple overview:

1) Buy Cash Value Life Insurance. Overfund with your inheritance cash.
2) Add appropriate life insurance riders.
3) Fund your bank with your cash.
4) Finance your purchases with your bank money.
5) Recapture that money.
6) Repeat all the above.

The History

Banking with life insurance isn't a new strategy. In fact, people have been using life insurance as a bank dating back before the Civil War.

What You Should Do Now

It is quite possible that you have never considered the living benefits of life insurance as a bank concept. There are so many advantages to heirs and heiresses by using the U.S. tax code to your benefit.

Let's do a quick reality check on this opportunity. Infinite banking is really only an option if you:

- Are highly liquid. I do not personally recommend this for less than $900,000 liquid.
- You can meet the premium payments effortlessly.
- You are exceptionally financially disciplined.
- You are committed to a lifetime of personal financial management.

"The infinite banking concept is not new; it has just been reserved in secret and whispered about amongst high-net-worth families."

~ A Video on Tik Tok ~

SECRET #10:

Transferring Wealth

Wealth transfer is the transfer of wealth or assets to beneficiaries upon the death of the owner through financial planning strategies that often include wills, estate planning, life insurance, or trusts in a tax-efficient manner.

What You Need to Know

If you are an heir, heiress or inheritor, it is highly likely you received your newfound wealth via a financial vehicle, such as:

- Wills.
- Estate planning.
- Life insurance.
- A trust. (UTMA, UGMA, GRAT, etc. It is also likely many in your circle of influence have no idea what these acronyms stand for.)

See how lucky you are?

The History

In human history, there has never been a financial time like this. Many baby boomers and an increasing number of Gen X families are getting ready to transfer their legacies through estate plans, putting

America on the cusp of the largest wealth transfer in history.

According to projections, 68.4 trillion dollars will be transferred over the next 25 years, causing a transfer of wealth unparalleled in human history.

What You Should Do Now

It is prudent for you to begin understanding all you can about preserving your estate and transferring it to the next generation. I caution you to not rely solely on one person. Seek a team of tax advisors and trust attorneys, and get a really great life insurance person who believes that life insurance is for the living.

If you are stuck, reach out and we can help.

"The transfer of wealth is literally the movement of money from one person to another. It can be accomplished through trusts, wills, estate planning and never ever forget this—life insurance."

~ Jeff Arnold ~

SECRET #11:

Stealth Wealth

Stealth wealth is the secret legal contract most wealthy people use to quietly, discreetly, gather, accrue and transfer wealth.

What You Need to Know

Want to know about a legal contract that the really rich and wealthy use and how everyone can use it to gather, transfer and save wealth?

Have you ever heard about a financial legal contract that allows you to pay money into it and get all your money back if not used?

Are you interested in transferring large sums of money to others tax free?

Before I reveal it to you, firstly, you have to repeat after me so you can reprogram your mind from all the lies and deceptions about this very simple legal contract.

Ready?

Repeat after me, "Life insurance is for the living and transferring wealth."

Say it again. "Life insurance is for the living and transferring wealth."

This is the only section of this book where I will expand greatly on a product that is so misunderstood. Let me pose a few questions:

Why don't more brokers and bankers offer this?

(They don't collect fees or get paid on it OR they think life insurance is for dying.)

Why does my broker say life insurance is expensive?

(They don't understand you can get all your premiums back or the tax-free benefits of wealth transfer if something happens to you.)

How come more people don't talk about this?

Wealth whispers. Get in the right circles, and you will hear about it.

The History

What do these families' names have in common?

Rockefeller, Kennedy, Morgan, etc.

They all transferred massive wealth to their heirs, using life insurance.

What You Should Do Now

Visit: https://whisper.jeffarnold.com.

There are five primary reasons people buy life insurance, but the first one is only understood by the wealthy:

1. Wealth transfer.

2. Burial or final expenses.

3. Income replacement.

4. Retirement savings cash value.

5. Mortgage pay off.

SECRET #12:

Annuities: SPIA

An annuity is an insurance product that can provide a secure income stream for the rest of your life. Annuities can be structured into different kinds of instruments, which gives investors flexibility.

What You Need to Know

A Single Premium Immediate Annuity (SPIA) is a contract between you and an insurance company designed for income purposes only. Unlike a deferred annuity, an immediate annuity skips the accumulation phase and begins paying out income either immediately or within a year after you have purchased it with a single, lump-sum payment.

SPIAs are also referred to as immediate payment annuities, income annuities and immediate annuities.

The History

This annuity is the oldest type, dating back to the ancient Roman Empire. The word annuity comes from the Latin word, *annua*, which means annual payments. Roman soldiers received lifetime annuity payments as compensation for their service in the military.

What You Should Do Now

I find it wise for heirs and heiresses to "lock up" a portion of their inheritance in a SPIA. Firstly, it prevents them from squandering money in their youth due to its withdrawal penalties, and secondly, if the right annuity is purchased, it can satisfy the need for gains, tax benefits and probate-free estate distribution. Please note that annuities are not great vehicles for wealth creation, but they are exceptional products for tempering the impending avarice desires of heirs and heiresses.

Learn more at: https://spia.jeffarnold.com.

"People always live forever when there is an annuity to be paid them."

~ Jane Austen ~

SECRET #13:

Annuities: SPDA

An annuity is an insurance product that can provide a secure income stream for the rest of your life. Annuities can be structured into different kinds of instruments, which gives investors flexibility.

What You Need to Know

A Single Premium Deferred Annuity (SPDA) is best suited for people planning for retirement who are worried that they may run out of retirement savings and who have enough cash on hand to fund the up-front premium payment.

An SPDA requires only a single lump-sum payment to fund the product.

History

As a repeat of the last chapter's history, the word annuity actually comes from the Latin word, *annua*, which means annual payments. Roman soldiers received lifetime annuity payments to compensate for their service in the military.

What You Should Do Now

I find it wise for heirs and heiresses to "lock up" a portion of their inheritance in a SPDA.

Firstly, SPDAs may feature either a guaranteed interest rate or a rate based on a stock market index. If tied to stock market index, the return can include a floor of 0%, meaning the annuitant cannot lose money in a down market cycle. Secondly, as stated in the previous chapter, a SPDA also prevents heirs from squandering money in their youth due to its withdrawal penalties. And if the right annuity is purchased, it can satisfy the need for gains, tax benefits and probate-free estate distribution.

Learn more at: https://spda.jeffarnold.com.

"Keep calm and invest some of your money in an annuity."

~ Your Future Self ~

SECRET #14:

Taxes

Taxes are a compulsory contribution, levied by the government on inheritances, workers' income, business profits or added to the cost of some goods, services, and transactions.

What You Need to Know

I am certain you have heard the saying, "Nothing in life is certain except death and taxes."

Most heirs and high-net-worth people would find death to be much, much easier than the complicated and inconsistent tax statutes they must navigate.

In addition to income tax, you will be subjected to investment taxes, capital gains taxes, gift taxes, alternative minimum taxes, marginal taxes, excise taxes, property taxes plus the taxes you pay on every purchase you make.

As I am writing this, your elected officials also passed a bill to add even more staff to audit your taxes while making every member of congress exempt from audits. (Yeah, I know <shakes head, keeps typing>.)

As time progresses, more and unique taxes are bound to be levied upon you to separate an unstoppable desire to give more of what you have to others or to your government as they believe they know what's best for you.

The History

We can thank the Egyptians and Pharoah for collecting a tax equivalent to 20 percent of all grand harvest. Since then, governments have become more addicted to your money and have an insatiable appetite for more.

What You Should Do Now

It is no longer a suggestion but an imperative that you meet regularly and consult your tax advisor or CPA prior to any stock sales, distributions or investments.

I have witnessed many heirs and heiresses rush quickly into liquidating an investment without planning on the tax bite and then find themselves in a dire financial situation.

Get and seek tax advice often.

"Can a people tax themselves into prosperity? Can a man stand in a bucket and lift himself up by the handle?"

~ Winston Churchill ~

SECRET #15:

Build Your Own Wealth Transfer Blueprint

What would you do—if you knew you could not fail?

What You Need to Know

As we wrap up, let me challenge you to dream big, and build your very own wealth transfer blueprint. You have the ability to stand on the shoulders of those before you, who took time, energy and resources to give you a life they most likely never had.

Do not squander this advantage. **Dream big. Do something bold.**

What would you do, if you knew you could not fail?

In short, what will your wealth transfer blueprint look like? For now, let's refer to it as your Superpower.

What's your Superpower?

Your Superpower is surely something that excites you, something that you would do for no pay for long periods of time and consumes most of your waking thoughts.

You, being the fortunate person you are, have the ability to bring your Superpower to life more than most and create a unique, one-of-a-kind wealth transfer model.

The History

This section is for you to write your own history of wealth transfer and gift it to your own heirs, next generation, etc.

What does your blueprint look like?

What You Should Do Now

I have witnessed many heirs embrace their wealth and focus on giving back to humanity, helping the needy, teaching inner-city schools, providing free legal help, starting their own empires, etc.

I have also witnessed that wealth can produce indifference, unrealistic expectations and a less than contributing member of society.

Find your Superpower, and take advantage of the life you have been given. You are in the company of a fortunate few. Always, always remember to thank the people or do something in honor of those who made this life possible for you.

"No one is like you,
and that my friend,
is your Superpower."

~ Jeff Arnold ~

Ways to Work With Me & RIGHTSURE

Over the last few pages, we have covered quite a few topics that may have you wondering about some of the concepts.

While the subject matter was intentionally short to keep readers engaged, if you have questions, keep reading to see how we can work together.

Helping consumers understand insurance and financial products has been my life's calling for more than 30 years.

Through my firm, RIGHTSURE, the most awarded insurance firm in North America, we have helped over 100,000 policyholders. Known for our Famously Friendly Humans, we insure everything from pets to jets, homes and drones, and all things in between.

Below, I offer three distinct opportunities to work with our exceptionally trained and famously friendly humans at RIGHTSURE and me personally.

Our RATESURE platform helps consumers maximize discounts and beat insurance company rate increases by leveraging our proprietary discount discovery technology.

https://ratesure.rightsure.com

Our Private Client Group offers the brightest Certified Personal Risk Managers, assisting mass affluent, high-net-worth families and family offices.

https://private.rightsure.com

Heirs, heiresses, and inheritors, kindly visit the URLs mentioned on the pages of this book to schedule personal reviews or to learn more.

https://jeffarnold.com

Thank you!

Jeff Arnold

About Jeff Arnold

Jeff has been called a thought leader and global ambassador for the financial and insurance industry. This pleases his mother and shocks his wife.

He writes and speaks on helping heirs, heiresses and inheritors get excited about the really cool things they can do with their money.

Jeff is the author of six books with five of them holding #1 or Best-Selling status.

His articles on agency management best practices have been published in numerous leading industry publications.

Jeff loves to speak to anyone about prolonging and enhancing their inherited wealth. He often speaks in small conference rooms, large conventions, company off-sites, impromptu Zoom calls and to the field mice behind his desert home.

To learn more about Jeff, visit:

https://jeffarnold.com

https://www.linkedin.com/in/rjefferyarnold

About RIGHTSURE

Known for its Famously Friendly Humans, RIGHTSURE helps consumers insure everything from pets to jets.

By using a unique, client-centered approach combined with superior technology, RIGHTSURE presents clients with a wide range of insurance options backed by a seamless purchasing process.

Headquartered in Tucson, Arizona, this tiny firm is disrupting the entire insurance ecosystem by leveraging, artificial intelligence, chatbots, predictive analytics and psychographic buying trends.

Recently heralded as the Most Awarded Insurance Firm in North America, recent 2022 awards are:

- 2022 Insurance Employer of the Year; *Insurance Business America*

- 2022 North American Insurance Firm of the Year; *FM Global Magazine*
- 2022 Spectrum Award of Excellence in Customer Satisfaction (six straight years); *City Beat News*®
- 2022 Leading Insurtech of the Year; *The Executive Headlines*
- 2022 Most Admired Innovation Driver in Insurtech; *The Silicon Review*
- 2022 Five Star Insurance Brokerage Winner; IBA North America
- 2022 Ultimate Tech-Blended Insurance Operation; *The Business Fame*
- 2022 Most Awarded Insurance Firm of the Decade; *The Enterprise World*
- 2022 Top 10 Most Disruptive Businesses; *Fortunes Crown*

Other Books by Jeff

Jeff is the author of six books with five of them holding #1 or Best-Selling status on Amazon, including:

- *The Art of the Insurance Deal*
- *How to Beat Your Insurance Company*
- *Tech-Forward, Tech-Enabled or Tech Shackled: Which Are You?*
- *Insurance Evolved: INSURANCE 2025*
- *Moments With Mucka: Business Building Sessions*

Visit his author page at:

https://jeffarnold.com/amazon

Made in the USA
Middletown, DE
31 October 2024

63128846R00052